STRONG HEART

JESS ANSELMENT

Copyright © 2025 by Jess Anselment
All rights reserved. No part of this book may be reproduced in any manner whatsoever without written permission except in the case of brief quotations embodied in critical articles and reviews.
First Printing, 2025

Contents

Dedication — vii
Preface — viii

Part 1 — 1
  1 Slow, Slithering Fog — 2
  2 Stay Put — 3
  3 Little Owl — 4

Part 2 — 6
  4 Thick Skin — 7
  5 It Really Starts Here — 9
  6 I Had to be Awake — 10
  7 Wadded Up Bread — 12
  8 Searching for Fossils — 14
  9 Pulse — 16
  10 Calloused and Numb — 17
  11 Good Girl — 18
  12 Oil Spill — 20
  13 Growling Beast — 23
  14 Failing — 24
  15 Transparent — 26
  16 Couch and Quilt — 27

17 I Already Knew	28
18 Belly-Breathing	29
19 Soft Thud	31
20 See Her Scars	32
21 Fiercely and Infinitely	33
22 Rest Softly	34
Part 3	35
23 Appointment	36
24 Doom Scrolling	37
25 I'll Wait	38
26 Closing Door	40
27 The Extent	41
28 It Hasn't Worked Out	42
29 Hovering and Apologizing	44
30 Lunch	45
Part 4	46
31 Brewing and Stewing	47
32 A Student of Soil	48
33 Brutality	50
34 Erratic Arrhythmia	51
35 Fading and Dwindling	52
36 A Little, Intrusive Thought	54
37 Grime of My Gratitude	55
38 Mom Things	57
39 Bounce Back	59
40 A Note to You (Yes, You)	60
Part 5	61
41 Muddy Puddle Ball Pit	62

42 Mud Goop Rubber Boot	64
43 Yuck-Stuff	65
44 Trail of Splats	67
Part 6	69
45 Swirl and Snap	70
46 Growing Stuffs	71
47 Hard Freeze	72
48 Another Gust	73
49 Hold the Line	75
50 Lovely Rot	76
51 Another Gust II	77
Part 7	79
52 Knees of My Jeans	80
53 Catchy Rhythm	81
54 Replant	83
55 Crawling Across and Covering	84
56 Butt in the Mud	85
57 Jellyfish	87
58 Butterfly Heart	89
59 Carrot Ball	90
60 Yes, a Carrot Ball	91
61 She's Waiting for You	92
Part 8	94
62 Forging Paths	95
63 Red-Hot Iron	96
64 Fall, Drift, or Pop	97
65 Snap, Clip, Nope	98
66 My Friend, Nicole	99

67	Magic Eye I	101
68	Magic Eye II	104
Part 9		105
69	Old Stone	106
70	I am a Statue	107
71	Freeze Person	109
72	Not a Side Quest	111
73	Wounds and Scars	113
74	Happy Pipe Dream	115
75	Strong Heart	117

All These Photos	119
Notes	120
About the Author	121

For King Ranch and Little Foot, the most beautiful pieces of my heart.

Preface

Years ago, my family and I left the city behind, trading its familiar hum for the quiet expanse of a country property in what felt like the middle of Nowhere, Texas. A decade has passed, and our lives have transformed as profoundly as the world itself.

For years, I kept a blog, tracing the ways country life reshaped my perspective—as a woman, a mother, and someone well-acquainted with both anxiety and chronic illness.

Looking back on this journey, I'm struck by how unrecognizable the world has become. A quiet unease lingers in the air—a shared anxiety, a collective sickness we all seem to carry. It feels as though we're waiting—breath held, hearts unsteady—for news that may never come. Plans feel fragile, commitments daunting, and even sleep offers little refuge.

That's why I'm publishing this small collection. I need a near-daily reminder that my heart is strong. And with this shared web of nerves I believe we're all plugged into, I thought perhaps you, reader, might benefit from that reminder, too.

I wrote some of these pieces eight years ago, some five years ago, and some just yesterday. There are themes here that once felt shocking but now seem muted by a relentless news cycle. That scares me.

Place your hand over your chest, close your eyes, and feel the steady rhythm of your heart. We all have one—every single one of us. It beats on, whether we acknowledge it or not. This collective rhythm, I believe, has become disconnected from ourselves and each other for far too long.

With your hand still over your heart, take a long breath in, all the way to the bottom of your belly. Hold it there for a moment. Then, as if it's the strongest magnet in the world, let all the darkness attach itself to your exhale and release it into the air—a personal smoke signal letting the world know that like a majestic mother bear, you're ready to hold your heart both tenderly and ferociously as we move through this chaotic time.

Be a parent to your inner child—the one who used to look up at the sky with wonder. Remember the first time you saw a shooting star, or the moment you learned that caterpillars become butterflies. Recall how incredible it felt to learn that a blue whale's heart weighs nearly 400 pounds. Wrap yourself in a blanket and watch a cartoon when you feel ill. Grab an extra cookie. Hug yourself tightly, especially when you're sad or scared.

Your heart is incredible. It is strong. It is valued. It is human. It is you.

May love and peace find and surround you, my friend.

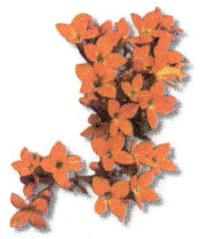

STRONG HEART

Part 1

Hoot hoot.

1

Slow, Slithering Fog

My favorite time:
the darkest,
heaviest sky before dawn

when fog lurks around,
low on the ground,
like a slithering dragon
on the prowl.

Standing in the living room,
windows like gateways to
faint, familiar trees,

a small hoot echoes.

One owl, one hoot.
A somber one, although
I don't know why
she sounds so sad.

2

Stay Put

I've read before that most owls mate for life and in the tragic event that an owl's partner may die, the living one stays put in the safe place they've built, waiting to see if one day, their other will come home.

3

Little Owl

Is that solemn hoot an owl
alone, waiting, hoping that
her beloved hears her call?

Does she fear that her partner
is lost, trapped, or injured?
Too far away to hear her hoot?

Is her dear too scared or
too weak to hoot back?
Are they even alive, at all?

She hoots, she hoots.

She hoots until the black
slowly shifts to gray and
the morning birds begin.

Another night in a nest,
waiting, wondering, worrying.
Perhaps one day, she'll leave

and explore; maybe she'd find
her lost mate. Or maybe she'd
(all on her own) see the world
and all her glory from above.

But I don't think she knows
how to leave her nest;
it's where she hatched her eggs,
(or where she hoped to)

And it's safe here.
Is it safe out there?

Little owl, I wish you knew
you weren't alone. I wish I
could wrap you in a blanket
and comb your feathers
and tell you it's going to be
okay, but we both know...

Keep hooting, baby girl.
I'll listen, I promise.
I'll stand here and listen
to your calls until the day
that there are two hoots
or until the day
that there are none.

Either way, I'll be so proud of you.

Part 2

All those beating hearts.

4

Thick Skin

"*Thick skin*" is more than just an idiom, it's a survival mechanism; a shield against the world's sharpest blows.

You're told to have this when someone insults your cooking, or reveals that you didn't make the dance team because

well, you just aren't good enough.

As a hyper-sensitive person who is affected by everything, *thick skin* is both a foreign concept and a source of deep frustration. *Thick skin*

is a passing grade that everyone else has aced while I'm shuffling and rooting around through chicken-scratch, trying to make

sense of it. How can one cultivate "*thick skin*" if they're not born with it? I've been told that my sensitivity makes people uncomfortable.

Not having *thick skin* is a weakness to work out.

5

It Really Starts Here

It was 6:30 on a hot, Texas morning.
On my cell phone was a notification:
an email from another publishing company
to whom I'd recently submitted a short story.

The subject of the email was too ambiguous
to know its contents, but after many recent
rejections, I decided to wait a while to open it.
I didn't want to start another day with a *"no."*

6

I Had to be Awake

These days, in addition to brushing my teeth and
washing my face in the morning, I also liberally
apply SPF 50 all over my body knowing that any
amount of time outside will result in a wicked sunburn.

I used to try to tan, but I'm a girl whose pink skin freckles.
Tanning is a painful process that always ends in
blisters that pop and peel.

I also come from a long line of scarred,
fair-skinned relatives, who warn me of the
dangers of the sun. They ask if I can see their scars
and do I know that they could have prevented it
had they just worn sunscreen?

Of course, when you're young, skin cancer is
something that happens to people much older than you.
Two months ago, however, I noticed that one of the
larger freckles on my right arm had changed shape,
now looking more like a splat than a spot.

Also: today, I turned 30.

I stood in front of the mirror and slid sunscreen
all over me. In the middle of my chest, in this light,
I could see my breast bone and the inside edges of my
ribs. Skin is so thin there. Beneath the freckles, faint,

blueish green lines pumped in and out of my heart.
I thought of my heart beating—blood rushing in
and pulsing out. It had been nearly 5-years since I had
heart surgery. Well, technically I had a *cardiac ablation*.
Some people have been quick to point out that I
should refer to it as a *procedure*, not a *surgery*.

I developed an arrhythmia when I was 24.

It got out of hand for reasons that doctors could not
figure out, to the point where I'd pass out walking up
stairs, if I got too hot, or if I stood up too quickly.

The morning I went in for the *procedure*, I found out
that I'd need to be awake so that my heart would behave as
"normally" as it had been—not affected at all by anesthesia.

I had to be awake.

7

Wadded Up Bread

I've been asked before if the surgery was painful and my response is always,

Yes, it was painful.

It was beyond painful.
I guessed that back in time,
this was what it felt like to
have a sword slide through
your chest during a dual
only without an opportunity
to protect myself.

I just laid naked under
stadium lights with 13 doctors
and nurses around me as nerve
endings in my heart were
quite literally burned away.

For days, my heart was swollen.
I discovered that wadding up

pieces of bread into dense balls
of dough and slowly swallowing
them was a cheap and easy massage
for the hurting walls of my heart.

8

Searching for Fossils

I placed a hand over my chest,
    the sunscreen cool in my palm,
and rubbed in slow circles.

Since that *procedure*, I've kept an
open dialogue with my heart.
I have pep talks with her.
I remind her what she's been
through when she's down.

After that cardiac ablation,
heartbreak meant something
completely different to us.

I ask her sometimes if she's doing alright.
For the most part she is, but she worries.
She worries about our kid and
how we're supposed to mother him
in a way that sets him up for success.

Her and I were bullied as children

and we just took it.
We didn't like confrontation
and I suppose we still don't—
(us still avoiding it at almost any cost)

Standing up to bullies or even
telling grown ups about being bullied
was a straight-shot path to confrontation.

So we kept quiet and waited for the day
to end when we could go home and play
with our beagle and dig holes in the yard
in search of dinosaur fossils.

9

Pulse

She worries about men with guns
because there are many days
where that's the only news story.

She didn't want to go to the movies
with her family because she kept
thinking about the Pulse nightclub
(it having happened only a few days prior)

She thought about Aurora.
Sandy Hook.
San Bernardino.

She thought of the young man
who texted his mom right before he died.

10

Calloused and Numb

She worries that things like mass shootings
and bullying and distant wars are
so common these days that we're all
becoming calloused to them and somehow,
we're supposed to raise a kid in all this.

Thick skin, I suppose.

But thick skin doesn't take away the mother's grief
when that last, heart-wrenching text came through.
Thick skin doesn't feed and house and embrace the
hundreds of thousands of people displaced
from forever wars. Besides thick skin, what can we do?

What are Syrian parents doing for their children
whose homes have been reduced to rubble?
Bullying is the least of their worries, but then again,
I'm sure it still happens. And hurts, just as badly.
All those hearts beating and beating...

11

Good Girl

I slid the sunscreen across the pale caps
   of my shoulders and down my biceps,
which I flexed to remind myself that there was strength there.
I avoided that little spot in the crook of my elbows
where I can very clearly see my veins because for some reason,
when I touch that spot, I feel a tickle deep down in my ears.

I don't know how to make her, my heart, stop worrying.
I don't know how to grow *thick skin.*
I've tried meditating.
Medication.
Therapy.
Even prayer.

But still, she worries.
I try my best to trust her strength
and remind her of it when she's lost sight of it.
She has, after all, survived torture under
bright lights in that surgery.

Good girl.

Buck up.

In the bedroom, my phone buzzed with some
new notification and that reminded me of the
email I hadn't opened.

Every single aspiring writer
who wants to make anything of it is
told that they have to have "thick skin"
and that rejection is all a part of it.

They're told to just keep going.
Move on to the next.
They've all been through it and so will you.
It's a rite of passage.
We all need to have thick skin.
It's good for you.

In my reflection, I remind myself of this.

*"Buck up, girl. You keep going. Thick skin.
Think of that anonymous message you got
on your blog telling you that your words
touched this random person you've never
met and that she loved the way the world
looked through your eyes."*

*"Remember how you cried in that grocery store
parking lot after reading this anonymous person's
message and you called your mom to tell her about it?"*

12

Oil Spill

That was the same parking lot
　　from which I called my husband
sometime last winter, shaking.

It was bitterly cold outside—
the kind of cold that whips
at your face like broken glass.

As I walked out of the grocery store
with my son in the basket's seat,
my eyes were drawn to the large,

muscular calf of a man in front of me.
He wore red and orange shorts
and a gray hoodie that fit him too tightly.

On his left calf,
wrapping around the entirety of it,
was a bold and black swastika.

It growled from his leg,

flexing with every step.
My kid was facing towards me *(luckily)*

(not that he'd know what it was...but still...)

There it was,
oozing out of his leg like oil leaking
from a rig in the Gulf of Mexico.

I realized then that I'd never seen a
swastika outside of books or films.
I stopped, there on the ramp

in front of the grocery store,
and watched the four-legged creature
attached to the man in shorts

march angrily towards the
sea of cars. The hair on my neck
tingled at the roots.

I looked around to see if anyone else
had noticed it too, but if they had,
I couldn't tell.

The swastika, along with its host,
cut through a few rows of cars
before sinking down

into a fancy, white sedan:
a stark-white sedan *(I don't know cars)*
with chrome rims that glistened.

He drove away (too quickly for
parking lots) as the engine
boomed in my bones.

13

Growling Beast

A real-life swastika on a real-life person.
    And he was proudly displaying it.
He *wanted* that tattoo to be seen.
He *wanted* to walk through a grocery store with it.
He *wanted* to be cold with it and flex it
and peel away loudly and dangerously in his car with it
like a growling beast asserting its dominance.
--

Back in the now, I tried to reach sunscreen
as far down on the backs of my shoulders
as my arms could reach.
My rib cage lifted when I did this
and I could see straight through it.
I could see the pulse right above my collar bones;
a tiny little bump, bump, bump.

14

Failing

The man with the swastika,
    from behind,
  seemed like a younger man.
  He couldn't have been much older than me

(today I am 30)

  and truly, I thought that
  that kind of hatred was dying out,
  and that *my* generation
  was bringing love back
  into a torn apart world.

  I wanted to believe that so badly.
  My heart did, too.
  We were children after segregation.
  We were children who learned
  about the holocaust,
  about slavery,
  about how we're all equal,
  and how wrong humanity had it before.

We learned in school how
power and money can corrupt
world leaders and so it was
our responsibility to do better.
It was our obligation,
as a human race,
to love as hard as we could,
otherwise, we'd fail.

That man in the parking lot made me feel like we were failing.

15

Transparent

Done applying sunscreen,
    I pulled a shirt over my head,
walked into the bedroom
and glanced over at my phone—
the green light in the corner calling me
to come back and check the notifications.

I thought about just getting it over with—
swallowing that "no" from the publisher's
email, but decided I wanted coffee first.
Thick skin, remember? Just keep going.

(But I *don't have* thick skin;
I can see right through it.)

16

Couch and Quilt

I sat on the velvet, purple couch in my living room.
An old friend who no longer talks to me
gave me this couch several years ago. Over the back of it

hangs a quilt that was made by a different friend's mom:
another friend, with whom I no longer have a relationship.
I sipped my coffee—my legs balled up beneath me

as I gazed out the window, watching my hens peck
for bugs in the yard. They scratched and nibbled
and I wondered about those two, old friends:

the purple couch and the mom quilt.
Neither of those relationships ended well or mutually.

At the bottom of my cup of coffee were some straggling grounds.
They were vulnerable, damp, cold, and confused.
With the tip of my finger, I wiped them onto my shirt.

17

I Already Knew

With a defeated sigh, I finally looked at
the home screen of my phone,
(my phone's background was a picture of my
wide-eyed donkey named Bunny).

The email envelope in the corner called for me.
Bunny the donkey, I'd decided, was smiling at me.
On the other side of that picture was probably
me dangling a carrot.

I tapped the notification.
*"Thank you for your submission,
however, this piece is not for us..."*

I stopped reading and turned off my phone.
Tears stung my eyes, but quickly, they stopped,
as the reel of *"you already knew this would be the answer"*

ran through my mind.
I did. I did know it was the answer.
Buck up. Thick skin.

18

Belly-Breathing

From his nursery, my son started to whimper,
    so I tossed my phone onto the bed
and went to pull him from his crib.

He smiled at me sleepily when I walked in,
reaching his arms for mine. I picked him up.
He rested his curly head on my shoulder.

I still love his smell. It's no longer new-born,
it's just him. Caring for him
sometimes makes me cry.

He's just so…so….

gosh I don't think there's a word.
He's my son. A piece of me.
The very best and most beautiful piece of me.

My heart reached for his, as she always does.
Sometimes, I think they actually communicate
through our chests. I carried him back into my room

and stood over my phone. It no longer blinked green,
but instead, was black and blank.
On my shoulder, my baby started to drift back to sleep,

so I laid on my bed, holding him against my chest.
His breath moved quicker than mine, but deeper.
His breath moved all the way down to the bottom of his belly

and I wondered...

at what point do we, as adults,
stop regularly belly-breathing?
It's just so shallow these days.

19

Soft Thud

I pulled my own breath down into my belly,
    allowing my heart to thump three full times
before exhaling. She liked it after she got used to it.

So did I.

I reached for my phone and opened the email again.
*"Thank you for your submission, however,
this piece is not for us. Don't feel bad, though;
this is a reflection of our aesthetic, not your quality."*

I laid back then, tossing my phone to the side.
It slid off the mattress and landed on the carpet
with a soft thud. I laid there and I cried, although
I wasn't sad. It was just another no.

But still, I cried, wishing I knew
how to form *thick skin* to make the
disappointment go away,
or at least, not sting so much.

20

See Her Scars

My heart played in the depth of my deep breath
as my small son's sleeping and breathing body
rose and fell on top of them.

I do not have thick skin and I'm beginning to wonder
if I ever will. I still don't like confrontation and I am
incredibly intimidated by things like hateful tattoos and guns.

I suppose I do have a strong heart, though.
I know that because I can see right through my
skin and into her. I can see all her scars from all those
burns and she really does wear them proudly.

21

Fiercely and Infinitely

She worries, but she hasn't stopped yet.
    And she hasn't stopped enjoying things
like deep breaths and donkeys and writing.

She hasn't stopped thumping for things she loves,
like her small son and her sweet partner.
She loves fiercely and infinitely. Gosh, sweet heart,

am I grateful for every last beat you've struck.
30 years, you and me. It's you who's brought me this far.
It's you who's held onto the relationships that matter.

It's you who doesn't lose hope even when we're hurt,
when we're rejected, or when we're intimidated.
It's *you* who reminds *me* that there are good

people in the world and that fear is only
what you allow. It's you who is the strong one and
the one I will follow so long as you'll have me.

22

Rest Softly

Little, strong heart,
    perhaps if I've got you
then I can stop worrying
over *thick skin*.

Maybe we can rest
softly in our sensitivity
and be grateful for depth.

Part 3

Chronic Illness.

23

Appointment

I stumble off an elevator 15 minutes late for an appointment.
Out of breath, I take my place in line, wondering if I should
craft an elaborate excuse for the woman at the check-in counter
or if I should just be honest that it's for no other reason than

having miscalculated the time it would take to get here.
A web-spun story could make me seem more responsible
than the truth: that I just didn't think it through all the way.
I'd hate for her to think I simply and sillily messed up.

I tell her I'm sorry I'm late and thankfully, there's no opportunity
to provide an excuse or reason, so the decision is made for me—
I remain mysteriously late. She says it's okay, that there was a
cancelled appointment after mine if I wouldn't mind waiting.

Of course I wouldn't mind and thank you for not charging
the $50 fee for missing my originally scheduled appointment.
I take a chair in the waiting room in the corner by the window,
still out of breath with sweat rolling down my back.

24

Doom Scrolling

As I wait, I scroll my phone:
doom scrolling, it's called.

Another school shooting.
Three children dead.

Wasn't there one yesterday?
Or was that the day before?
Or maybe this is the same one
with more information?

Yesterday's or last week's or
last month's or last winter's
mass shooting is old news,
blurred with all the others.

All the others.

25

I'll Wait

It's been 30 minutes and I haven't been called back. I debate whether or not I should ask the receptionist if she has any idea how much longer it will be until my rescheduled appointment. I have a video conference for my day job scheduled in a bit and now that I've *diligently* calculated the travel times in my head, I know exactly the last minutes I have to leave here, commute home, and hop on that call; we're not too far away from that time.

But see, she's already accommodated me for my flub-up; I hate to ask how long and seem impatient or ungrateful. I decide to wait a little while longer. These appointments are hard to reschedule. Plus, I've met my health insurance's out-of-pocket max for the year—if I get rescheduled after the new year, it'll cost so, *so* much more. This is an important appointment, too. I've been through a host of new tests and we will go over those tests today, talk options, and hopefully create a plan to manage this chronic illness.

I'll wait. I'll count to 100 by tapping each one of my fingers to my thumb and then I'll do it again. And maybe again.

I tap my phone back on and the school shooting pops up.
"Sandy Hook should have been enough," commented some guy;
I think about how some people don't believe it even happened.

26

Closing Door

This morning, I kissed the top of my son's head as he bounced off to school with his bright green backpack and his little mask.

His curls smell like his shampoo and as the door closed behind him, he said, "I love you too, mom."

27

The Extent

The nurse calls me back, oh thank goodness.
After taking my vitals, she says the doctor
will be in shortly. I'm within 20 minutes now
of having to leave in time to make this video call
and I think, okay, worst case scenario, I can
conference in from my car in the parking lot,
assuming I have enough internet connection.
I won't have my notes, but I can manage...

10 minutes have passed and still no doctor.
Do I send an email to the participants
of the call saying I might be late? I've had to
cancel / reschedule / show up late / leave early
because of my stupid health and it makes me
feel so unreliable and burdensome. Most of them,
(my digital colleagues), know I have health issues,

but most of them will never know the extent of it—
heck, *I* don't even know the extent of it.
I hate being a burden.

28

It Hasn't Worked Out

My child's class lines up and switches
buildings a few times a day to go
to the gym, to recess, to art, to the library...

It's in those times, when their little line bobs
along the covered sidewalks that I worry
the most about shooters. In a classroom,

teachers these days are versed in how to
barricade doors, but what about when
they're in little lines in the hallway or

out in the open? Or on the playground?
And how do you explain to a child that
there are people in the world who could

show up with a gun and start firing at will?
What do you do if you see it? When I was in school,
it was tornadoes we worried about and practiced

drills for and as my mom tells me, when it was

her age, they practiced drills for nuclear holocaust.
At least tornadoes don't do it on purpose.

I begin to draft an email on my phone that
I'll be late and calling in from my car.

They (my son's class) will be going to lunch soon.
He's asked me a few times to come have lunch
with him and I keep telling him I will. I want to,

it just hasn't worked out yet.

I begin to type:
"I'm so sorry, but I have a doctor's appointment that's
running longer than expected, so I will probably be
late for this call and dialing in from my car..."

29

Hovering and Apologizing

I look at the drafted email and reword it a few times. All I can think about is how I want to hug my kid and smell his little curls and tell him that I love him.

I can hear the doctor talking to another patient in the hall but now, it's too late. The time to leave to make this video meeting has passed and I'm still sitting here with my thumb hovering over this drafted email where I'm apologizing.

I'm always apologizing.

30

Lunch

I delete the whole
email and start over.

*"Unfortunately, I am unable
to make this call today.
Please let me know when
you're able to reschedule
and I will update the calendar."*

Send.

I slide my phone into my pocket
as the doctor knocks on the door
and steps in with my big file.
I scoot forward in my chair, anxious,
but also...okay.

After this appointment,
I'm going to surprise my
son with lunch.

Part 4

Mind your spoons.

31

Brewing and Stewing

It's mid-afternoon. I'm standing just inside my backdoor, still holding onto the handle, wondering if I should call it a day on yard-work or if I have it in me to continue.

In southeast Texas where I live, we've had a record-breaking summer in which the temperatures have soared far above 100°F, while also dragging us through a torturous drought.

My little pocket of the world is typically a swamp. I love it. Many people have told me that with humidity levels often hovering at 90% and above, it'd be a nightmare to live here,

but I quite like it. I feel moisturized, soft, and privy to a secret world that brews and stews in the primordial muck—the creatures who crawl out of it being vibrant, colorful, and

smart, but overwhelmingly misunderstood. This drought, however, has left us brown, crispy, and cracked where normally, we'd see mud, mushrooms, and moss. Finally though, after three months, it rained.

32

A Student of Soil

I am an avid gardener,
although I'm no expert.

I fiddle around with
my gardens each year

learning something new
about the soil,

companion planting,
disease, or composting

that I try to carry
with me to the next

season, hoping that
one year, I'll finally

cultivate that most
picture-perfect,

secret garden
with sprawling vines

and little, winding
stone paths.

33

Brutality

The brutality of this summer,
however, has left little room
for gardening success. No amount
of water, shade, or pampering has

stopped my plants from cooking
under the hot, Texas sun. Even
my easy-going guys, like Lantanas
and Impatiens have struggled to flower.

I've still tried, though. I've tried every single day

to touch the plants in my garden,
moisten their roots, trim the dead
from their stems, and keep some

semblance of a pollination station for the
neighborhood birds, bees, and butterflies.

34

Erratic Arrhythmia

So today, after it rained two days ago,
I've tended heavily to my garden in hopes
that I might revive the struggling parts of her.

With dirt under my fingernails, garden gunk stuck
to me in lines of sweat, and my hands too shaky
to type the code of my phone to open it, I decide
that perhaps I should call it a day. I do, after all,
have a heart condition which I can feel is flaring—

its palpitations are so strong I can't hear anything
but the erratic pulse of that bigeminy arrhythmia.

Dun duuuuuuuh dun. Dun duuuuuuuh dun.

35

Fading and Dwindling

Like my mostly dead garden, it's been months since I've watered the proverbial soil of my writing. I've left it to slowly die on the sidewalk like an

earthworm simply trying to cross the sidewalk from one patch of grass to another.

Do you ever see that when you're out for a walk— dead earthworms who have tried to cross the sidewalk but got cooked along the way?

And if it's a path you walk often, do you notice that these little creatures who were just trying to dig around in the cool dirt and do worm things so quickly

become a fading smudge of their former selves until there's nothing left at all? I hate it. I hate the idea of dying that way.

If you see an earthworm on the sidewalk, do it a favor: pick it up and bring it to the other side.

Lord knows they do a ton for us with little to no return.

But like the sad decay of an earthworm or a garden, my writing
(and most of my creative endeavors at all) has dwindled
into a smudge of its former self.

I've just not felt inspired.
I've not had anything I've wanted to share
or stories I've wanted to tell.

36

A Little, Intrusive Thought

I've had conflicts.
 I've had successes.
I've had loss.
I've had surprises.

I've had good and bad,
big and small,
somethings and nothings
and everything in-between,

but along the way,
I've not had writing.

It's dead beneath the
brutality of the season
and all I can hope is
that next season,

I'll have brought the
lessons of this year
to build into the next.

37

Grime of My Gratitude

I'm too dirty from yard-work to sit on a piece of furniture,
so I decide to use my last few spoons to shower—
to rinse off the grime of my gratitude that the sky finally fell.

Just when I thought I ought to dig up my whole garden until
nothing but empty lines of dried-up dirt remained, it rained.
Likewise, I've been tossing around the idea of bringing my

writing endeavors to an end. I've thought it might be time
to rip up her roots, till the land, and start something new.

I don't know. I sometimes feel like one of those earthworms
who started a big journey across the sidewalk with hopes and
dreams, only to have stalled halfway there, burning under the
viciousness of an unrelenting sun while everything and

everyone else p a s s e s m e b y.

Do you ever feel that way?
Passed up?
Walked over?

Helpless?
Smudge-like?

But it's got to rain, right? At some point, it's got to rain.
It literally did the other day and it gave me so much joy to know
that my efforts in a roasting garden all summer were worth it.

I think sometimes I worry that my efforts elsewhere
won't have that return. But I wonder, would it be that bad?
All summer long, I've been pushing a giant stone uphill,
hoping that the roots and established parts of my garden
would survive and maybe, *(just maybe)*, they actually would.

The rain gave me hope.

But what other stones are worth pushing and for how long?
When do you call it?
Do you ever call it?

38

Mom Things

Anxiety thrives in those big questions
with no concrete or blanket answers,
and it's that bubbling, anxious bog where
we should stop and ask ourselves,

"What can I control in this situation?"

I can't control the rain.
I can't control the cycle of life.
I can't control literary agents or publishing houses.
I can't control the changing climate.
I can't control trends in industries.

I can only control myself and my responses to things...

like enjoying this moment of hope because it rained.
I can be grateful that I had the energy today
to work outside and be glad that I know my heart's
limits when I reach them. That, I can control.

I can take a shower, dry my hair, and do my day job

all before my kiddo comes home from school
and when he's here, I can help him with his
homework, play video games with him, fix dinner,

Mom things.

39

Bounce Back

The other things?
Well, I suppose
that's where we change
constantly and adapt.

Easier said than done—
this swampy place has
crumbled under this
excruciating summer.

But she'll bounce back.
Swamps can do anything.

40

A Note to You (Yes, You)

I hope you're doing okay, you person reading this.
I really do. I hope you're taking care of yourself,
setting boundaries, minding your spoons,
trimming the dead stuff from your branches,
and trucking on with hope that the rain will come.

It will.
It always does.

In the meantime, try to slow down.
Don't feel bad if you need to do less in a
world telling you that more is always better.

Drink more water. Go outside.
Take a break. Tend to your roots.

Part 5

Expanding.

41

Muddy Puddle Ball Pit

For the third day in a row, it's pouring.
My grumpy donkeys huddle together
in the barn as the rain batters the tin roof
so loudly that it rattles my bones—it must
be deafening to their large, sensitive ears.

After piling their feeders with extra hay
in lieu of typical grazing time, I pull the
hood of my rain coat over my head and
slide the barn door shut behind me.

Like a million pellet guns, the drops strike.

My ducks scatter around the yard, rain wicking
from their slick feathers. Like children in a
ball pit, they bounce and play gleefully in the
muddy puddles. The chickens on the other hand,
band together in one of their coop's nesting boxes,
grumpier than the donkeys—wide, feathery floofs.

I make sure they've got plenty of dry food, then

check to make sure none of my little plants
are flooded, and finally check on the part of the
fence that leans too far when the ground is soft
before seeking refuge under the covered porch.

42

Mud Goop Rubber Boot

Like a dog after a bath, I shake as much
water off of myself as I can. To nearly the
top of my rubber boots, mud goops like
raw brownie batter so I sit down on an
empty milk crate—(a crate I've had forever,
although I'm not sure where it came from?)—
and slide them off with a suctiony slurp.

43

Yuck-Stuff

I forgot to bring towels outside and so until I'm not dripping, I'll stay seated on the milk crate. A shiver runs down my spine and echoes through my limbs. It's cold—too cold for East Texas. Low 40s and wet. I briefly consider wrapping the grill cover around me but that's also where I've seen not one, not two,

but three different black widows over the past year. So, nevermind. (I guess black widows prefer their meals grilled? Ha.)

The cold scurries up and down my spine like a mouse; chilly, little paws tick-tick-ticking. The shivers follow the rhythm of my heartbeat: pangs like beating drums ripple back and forth. A puddle of my dripping self has formed around the milk crate— its rounded edges creep outward with every drop, latching onto

stray bits of dirt and mulch. The puddle grows and grows, swallowing all the grit around me, the mucky water now littered with specs of dirty farm junk. The temperature's become painful and at this point, it's swallowed me whole. It would make sense to end this torture by going inside regardless of the dripping,

but I've become enamored with this slowly e x p a n d i n g pool.
It just keeps growing. Of course I could end its growth any time;
I am in complete control of this particular puddle's fate.
Subsequently, I am in complete control of the fate of all the bits of
ground stuffs that one by one are being sucked into the edges and
then into the belly of the beast. It grows and it grows because

I'm allowing it to. I'm invested now. If I were to move, I'd step in it,
break it, free the yuck-stuff, and proceed on with my day as if this
thing I've created with my drippings and my time never existed and
then what would all the effort of sitting out here with this be for?
A fleeting, non-reconstructable yuck-stuff scene living
only in my memory?

44

Trail of Splats

Carefully, I stand.
I step delicately
over the yuck puddle
(which recoils a bit)
and as I walk towards
the door, a trail of
splats follow me.

Wet socks leave
footprints across the
cement and even
after I strip down
and wrap up in a
thick throw,
dampness remains.

Even now, in the
soft blanket, my
toes and fingers
are pruned and
my guts still

shiver and shake.

I pull the blanket
tighter and wrap my
arms around myself.

Relax.

Try to relax.

Let your eyes
sink back in
their sockets.

Sweet girl, it's
okay. It's okay.
Come here, it's okay.

Part 6

The coming winter.

45

Swirl and Snap

It's dark out which by no means
means it is late. We have entered
that time of year where the sun falls

at 4:30PM, forcing us all into an earlier,
Pavlovian need to eat and bunk down
for the night, hours before we should.

I'm standing at the back window
watching patches of ground visible by
the lamp beside me.

Leaves
       swirl
              and
                     snap

as windchimes clash and clang.

I think the house is swaying.

46

Growing Stuffs

Although I can't see it, I'm looking in the direction of my garden. The weather forecast showed that tomorrow night, this swampy, little corner of the world would receive the first freeze of the year. (The low 20's kind of freeze.)

That kind of cold just isn't in my blood. Give me heat, humidity, air like a warm washcloth and like a fungus, I will slimily thrive.

I've become utterly obsessed with my shadowed garden out there. I spritz her. I fertilize her. I prune her. I talk to her. I harvest her. Homegrown edamame, green beans, perky, little tomatoes, peppers, onions, herbs of all kinds, rainbow wildflowers for the pollinators...

47

Hard Freeze

Alas, tomorrow night,
the hard freeze.
Hours of it., low 20s.
That's a death sentence
for my secret garden...
my sweet, sunny,
perfect little plants.

Sure, I'll cover them
with a warm blanket
and hope that somehow,
someway, they survive,
although I'm not optimistic.

I've also decided that
I will pluck some of the
larger tomatoes from their
stems, place them in a
sunny window and hope
they continue to ripen.

48

Another Gust

Another gust of wind whips the window and I sigh. What will I do now when I become over-stimulated or feel myself tumbling to a panic attack? For months, it's been the ritual of escaping to my garden which has tethered me down into quietude. My own, secret garden.

Only I have known what lies within its boundaries and there, I have found peace. My fortress of solitude. There's been a uniqueness to this place I've grown—this place that without my constant tinkering and attentiveness may have otherwise not succeeded and when I wake tomorrow, she'll have gone.

Streams of tears begin to roll down my cheeks and I have to laugh a bit. I don't think I've ever shed a tear over plants. What's wrong with me? But then the seal breaks and suddenly, I'm in a full on, blotchy, snotty cry.

I don't want to say goodbye.
I don't want to see her die.
I want her to continue to grow and

glow and reach for the sky. She's worked and tried so hard. She's overcome so much. She's created incredible things.

49

Hold the Line

I wipe my face and wonder
if I ought to make some tea
and turn on a dumb show to
distract myself from this
confusing and odd moment,

but I stop myself and
hold my place at the window,
staring into the all-too-lightly
illuminated darkness where
leaves flitter chaotically.

50

Lovely Rot

I wonder if my compost will freeze?
Compost is fascinating: the death
and rot and breaking down of once
living things that over time and digestion,
transform into unmatched nutrition
for future growth. What a circle of life.

Maybe that's what this whole garden thing is—
a breakdown of something in order to
make room for something new. A closing door.
An end but also not really. My hope is that
the soil will be healthier when I start a

new garden in the spring. Maybe she'll have
held onto some of her nutrients and maybe
after a till and a fold in of compost, she will
be ripe and ready to begin again.

51

Another Gust II

Another gust of wind whips
and although it's barely 5:00,
I decide to change into comfy clothes,
take my contacts out, and stare at
something for a while—the ceiling,
outside, or maybe some random show
that just makes some noise to fill space
so that the only room that's left is the
consideration of my own

rotting,

breaking down,

shifting,

dying,

grieving,

and regrowing

with something (hopefully) fuller, brighter,
and more fruitful on the other side.

I suppose that the important thing is that we're minding it.
We're giving it time. We're trying and we're taking care.
Most of all, I think it's important to admit that we,
like the seasons and the things that thrive within them,

change too.

We till.

We nurture.

We grow.

We die.

We breakdown.

We grieve.

We build again.

Part 7

Rake, rake. Dig, dig. Pull, pull. Brush, brush.

52

Knees of My Jeans

It's a chilly afternoon and I've decided to clear weeds and old roots from the garden in order to prepare for a new, spring crop. For more than two months now, I've let weeds and grass overtake my sad, little garden.

I pick a corner and kneel down to begin pulling up weeds. Dampness from the soil soaks into the knees of my jeans, but I don't mind. I start by raking the stringier weeds with my fingers which are tangled loosely across the top of the bushier and more deeply-rooted growth below.

Rake, rake rake.

Dirt gathers beneath my fingernails and what was a chilly afternoon has become quite warm with repetitive movements.

53

Catchy Rhythm

Row by row,
(whether planting
or clearing), there's
a natural rhythm
at work.

Rake the loose weeds.
Dig around stubborn ones.
Yank the deep roots.
Brush away the leftover.

Rake rake,
dig dig,
pull pull,
brush, brush.

Rake rake,
dig, dig,
pull, pull,
brush, brush.

One, two, three, four.
One, two, three, four.

Bit by bit and
breath by breath:

Rake, rake,
dig, dig,
pull, pull,
brush, brush.

54

Replant

Death always makes way
for new life.

Shares of heartache,
hurt, missteps, and much
like a garden, we fall

victim to poor management.

Unfortunate circumstance.

Neglect.
Distraction.
Propaganda.
All that.

55

Crawling Across and Covering

So here, squatting down
in the mud and the weeds
that thrive because of
neglect, I imagine that
the soil is life-giving light

and the weeds are darkness,
swiftly crawling across and
covering the richness and
space from which life, love,
and nourishment sprouts.

Rake, rake,
dig, dig,
pull, pull,
brush, brush.

56

Butt in the Mud

Gosh, there are weeds everywhere.
My hands are beginning to hurt
and the dampness from the ground
spreads like gel down my shins.

For the first time, I notice my
fingertips covered in tiny, red cuts.
Why didn't I wear gloves? It's so hot.

My heart rate has risen significantly
and I can no longer find my breath.
I try counting, but can't hold my
attention span to four anymore.

I pull my phone out of my pocket
and find the app which is connected
to the USB-sized monitor implanted
in my chest, right above my heart.

It's recording all the time,
but I'm supposed to report when I feel

abnormal things occuring, which is often
and especially when I do things like

squat down for too long. I sit back,
butt in the mud, and lean against the small,
picket fence as the app begins to record my
heart's rhythm which is heavy and fluttering.

The space around me vignettes and my fingers
and toes tingle, burn, then numb. I close my eyes
feeling the wet ground absorb into my jeans
and try again to find my breath.

Rake, rake,
dig, dig,
pull, pull,
brush, brush.
One, two, three…
One, two…
One, two, three.

57

Jellyfish

I can't get
the breath
to the bottom
of my lungs.

I try to relax
my gut, pelvis,
chest, and eyes,
and imagine
sinking a little
farther down
into the wet
ground.

Jellyfish gently
and repetitively
pulse through
the water.

My diaphragm
and breath

move in tandem
like a jellyfish
propelling itself
through the deep:

smoothly, silently
rhythmically, and
gracefully.

Blub, blub, blub
she goes...
soft, smooth,
and infinitely.

Blub, blub, blub,
through the blue.
Blub, blub, blub,
held by water.

58

Butterfly Heart

Once the flapping wings of my butterfly heart settles,
I open my eyes and lean forward onto my muddy knees.
My fingers and toes prickle with circulating blood as light returns.

I figure I ought to head in to get some water and rest,
but then something catches my eye. What is that?

59

Carrot Ball

Scrambling to my hands and knees,
I crawl to a tall, bright green growth
reaching delicately (and intentionally)
from the weeds. I trace my fingers down
the soft stems and carefully wiggle.

Easy...easy...(I'm pulling up oh-so-gently!)

When POP.
Oh my goodness.
I quite literally laugh.

A carrot ball.

A carrot ball
no bigger than a
ping-pong ball,
dangles
      from the
            proud leaves.

60

Yes, a Carrot Ball

Carrot ball and soon-after-discovered friends.

61

She's Waiting for You

I spent much of the rest of this day reclined on the couch with a big glass of water, imagining blooms of jellyfish pulsing through the deep.

How strange it must be to pulse endlessly through the darkness...

Blub, blub, pulse, pulse, on and on they go. Infinite, rhythmic movement.

I imagine the proverbial weeds that often stretch themselves across me and how somehow, someway, light manages to get through. Sure, sometimes, that

light goes undiscovered for a while, but it's there. It is. And certainly it's worth the blood, sweat, and pain to pull back the darkness and make way

for more light. Just start in a corner and
see what happens. Darkness breeds in
neglect. I'd say, get in; get your hands dirty.
Even if you don't find anything at first,

rake, dig, pull, and brush, anyway.

The process is still wonderfully meditative—
Afterall, you can't start a new garden without
first tearing up the old, deceased one.
In that death and chaos lies life
waiting for you; waiting to burst and bloom.

Part 8

Magic Eye.

62

Forging Paths

It's mid-afternoon on a mid-spring day here in East Texas. These rare, low humidity days are celebration-worthy and all the critters on the farm agree—them with their zoomies all over the yard. I'd run around with them too, if I could.

I'm out in the pasture with my donkeys, three. I don't take the time like I used to when I would just sit with them for hours. Sitting with animals who are as unsure of you as you are of them helps build mutual trust. It builds strong, solid foundations.

Literally, just sitting.

No phones. No timers. And what surprised me after doing this many times was how much it helped me get to know myself, too. I don't do this as much anymore because, well, I know these three donkeys through and through. Our daily routines are as set as the trails and paths they've carved all around the property.

63

Red-Hot Iron

I guess what I'd forgotten is
how much *I* needed the time.

To sit and feel grounded.
Timeless bouts of sitting,
being together...I have failed
to carve out that time.

What other basic needs
am I neglecting because
it's familiar or routine?

It doesn't have a red-hot iron
so I need not pay attention?
And could that be why I feel
like my tether's been clipped
and I'm drifting around in the
clouds like a lonely, lost balloon?

64

Fall, Drift, or Pop

I'm sitting on the ground, pine needles poking through my pants, crying a big, heaving, splotchy cry. I'm so tired of being tired.

Really, the metaphor of the lost balloon fits because how long can they float around up there by themselves before they either lose all their air and
>   fall
>   back
>   down
>   to
>   Earth?

Or drift t o o   f   a   r   ?

Or *POP?*

65

Snap, Clip, Nope

It's what chronic illness does to a person:
pushes them farther and farther away

and when everything they try to latch onto
is clipped away one by one, at some point,
there's nothing left to hold them down.

"Maybe this is where I belong," *snap*
"We found this, it might fit," *clip*
"This test should give us the answer" *nope*

I'm imagining those little static electricity balls
where the lighting dances around and around
desperately looking for something to connect to.

66

My Friend, Nicole

I spend the next hour or so
out in the pasture with my
donkeys, but after a while,
come in for a job that needs
my attention. A job that I like.

I've learned to make healthy
boundaries with this job and
it has connected me with some
compassionate, understanding,
and kind colleagues all over.

I often look forward to work
because it plugs me into being
human. As digitally connected
as we all are today, I feel like
our humanness isn't as connected

as it once was. Like sitting for
hours with my three donkeys,
how often do we get to do that

with each other? Just go for a
walk together? Picnic in the park?

Wander around the high-end
grocery store just to look at stuff,
knowing that everything is
too expensive but that lady might
be serving samples of smoked salmon
on aisle 12 so it's worth it?

An old high school friend and I
used to bring bags of navel oranges
to the park and sit on the swings
and eat them. I honestly can't remember
what she and I would talk about.

I don't know where she is today
or what she, Nicole, is doing
but I genuinely hope she's okay.

67

Magic Eye I

It's as if things have been too busy and too fast
to focus on any one thing. Life these days has felt
like one of those old Magic Eye images that used
to be in the newspapers: busy graphics that make
no sense until you can relax your gaze enough
to see a definable image pop up off the page.

I slide open the barn door and three sets of ears
are perked up high, no doubt, waiting for breakfast.
"Oh it's a good morning," I say in my sing-song voice
as I use a knife to cut the twine on a fresh bale of hay.
"It's a good, good morning for my good, good donkeys."
Three faces are hanging over the stall doors,
noses flared, and eyes wide.

It's so warm here.

The truth is, I have lots of stories I want to tell.
I want to tell y'all about going to Death Valley
and meeting real life wild burros—burros that are
descendants of those who built the American West;

about how old life is out there in those mountains.

I want to tell y'all about the Public Market in Seattle
where I had, hands down, the best champagne
I've ever had in my life with company that made me
smile so hard my cheeks hurt.

I want to tell y'all that in just a couple weeks time,
my very first book....*my* book...will debut.

I want to tell y'all about how it snowed the other day
and about how I had to run out to my garden and
harvest what I could before it froze too hard and
laughed when the only vegetable that actually grew
in the whole garden were three green beans.
Three.
Three beans.

I want to tell y'all about a weekend with old friends
where we sat around my kitchen table for hours
trying to play dominoes, but instead derailed over and over
into talking about life and how much it means to all of us
that our paths have crossed the way they have.
I want to tell y'all that my friends said some things to me
that resonated deep within my soul: they told me things
about myself that I hadn't realized. I can't quite process it.

I want to tell y'all all these things and more
but I just can't seem to relax my gaze enough
to describe the image that I know is hiding
somewhere in the busyness of this Magic Eye.

I finish mucking the stalls and stand in the barn

for a moment watching the donkeys eat their hay,
their tails swishing from side to side.

I'll head in soon where the coffee will have finished
brewing and Little Foot will likely be waking up.
I'll hold him and ask him about his dreams and
twirl his curly hair between my fingers. I'll watch
the way he uses his hands when he talks and
be so tickled that every day, his smile is looking
more and more like my own: crooked and showing
so much upper-gum.

68

Magic Eye II

I suppose that for now, it's okay if I don't see a single,
pronounced figure in the Magic Eye illustration:

maybe instead, right now, it's about appreciating
all the little shapes, textures, colors, and patterns

that swirl around themselves, especially in the peripheral.
That's how you spot wild burros, after all; you only notice

them out of movement in the corners of your eyes.

Or maybe, this isn't about a single, hidden image at all.
Maybe instead, it's about stepping back and watching

the kaleidoscope turn with images that shift and spin—
attention undivided so you don't miss a thing.

Part 9

Reach Out.

69

Old Stone

This morning, the air was thick and hung heavy over the ground, flies and grasshoppers rattling around in a floor of pine needles.

Here and there, the sun peeked through a web of thick clouds and it was bath-water warm. But now, as the afternoon tips towards sundown, a gray blanket coats the sky and I don't think I could point out where exactly the sun is if I tried.

The air's gone dry and the trees look like they would crumble if you so much as tapped their trunks. Old, fragile stone: everything looks and feels like old, fragile stone. A graveyard.

70

I am a Statue

I feel exactly like what it looks like outside right now:
an old statue unearthed in some new archaeological dig
which was once very strong, but time and circumstance
has stripped away her strength.

All the archaeologists handle with the utmost, latex-gloved,
careful hands because so much has broken off this statue already,
we wouldn't want to lose any more of it. If we did, it wouldn't
even be worth shipping to some museum, representing a long
forgotten and colorful past that I'm sure some people are
interested in learning about, but mostly I feel like something
that doesn't exist anymore.

And like a statue, I feel stuck.
Stuck in a pose that someone else crafted me into,
forever reaching my hands in the same direction,
clueless as to what could be behind me.

I'd ask to be turned to at least see what else is out there,
but that would risk breaking more of me. I think sometimes,
passerbyers look at the expression on my face and feel something,

but far and beyond, I feel that once I'm glanced at, I'm forgotten: just another ruin pieced together as best she can that once meant so much to people and now...

...well, now I'm behind glass panes watching everyone pass me by, reaching for them, but never having anyone reach back.

71

Freeze Person

I have a therapist and I love her
and I'll never, ever be ashamed
to admit my need for counseling
and neither should you.

I actually think the world
would be a much better place
if everyone went to therapy,
at least every once in a while.

I've described to her this weird place
where I feel frozen and lonely,
even though my friends and family
do continue to check up on me.

Like every little tinge I get in my
body right now sends me spiraling,
wondering, "how can it get worse?"
But beyond the conscious fear, stillness

(that I both crave and fear) allows

little bubbles to wiggle out and
make their way into my mind's eye,
popping and fizzing with relentless angst.

(what if, what if, what if?)

I'm feeling rejection, heartbreak, trust lost,
self-consciousness, and medical traumas in
ways that I haven't felt in a long time.
And I guess that's not that uncommon?

My therapist tells me that trauma can trigger
that fight/flight/freeze reaction and that can
release stress hormones and adrenaline exploding
everywhere, ultimately screwing everything up,

including trying to make space for healing.
Like a bird whose intricately woven a nest
gets suddenly knocked off the branch, sending
it tumbling; an explosion of gathered things.

I realized several years ago that I'm a
freeze person in most cases. I shut down.
I go cold. The blood drains from my body
and before I fully realize what's happened,

I am that statue behind the glass,
stuck forever in an expression of fear.

72

Not a Side Quest

I'm craving for someone to reach out towards my frozen, extended hand because at least then, I'll know I'm seen.

But when I jump out of the metaphor, I don't know what that looks like in real life. I don't know what I need.

I don't know what *we* as a whole society need. I feel lonely, scared, isolated, pessimistic, and not worth anyone's time,

(and that is a sad and pitiful admittance, but I don't think I'm alone in feeling this way, right? ...right?)

For some time now, I've been on what I thought was a side quest, but maybe it's the main objective of the game:

to pull back the covers on what it means to be soft in a cruel, competitive, world. I want to shine light on the parts

of us that our brain and society says aren't good enough even though I think most of us are doing our very best.

And our best should *always* be good enough. But it's hard to do that in a world that moves so, *so* fast.

No wonder we feel left behind.
Frozen. Passed by.

73

Wounds and Scars

Sometimes with healing, there's no movement
for so long that it feels like it's stopped and
now, this is the scar we're left with. This is it.

But sometimes, there so much movement so quickly
that your body shuts itself down in protest to
a scary, rapidly changing state of things.

Healing won't begin without stopping for a moment
to assess what it is we're actually dealing with.
The wound just rips right back open, even worse.

For many, many years, I've defaulted to the metaphor
that if you don't clean out a wound, it'll get infected
and won't heal the right way. It'll be so much harder

and so much more painful to try and go back after the
scar has formed to try and clean out all the gunk you
didn't deal with before, so handle it while it's fresh.

But if you miss that window, it's still worth it to slice

the scar open, dump some alcohol on it, swab it, stitch it, and tend carefully to it so it'll heal right this time.

74

Happy Pipe Dream

Earlier in this book, I mentioned the USB-sized monitor implanted above my heart—a "loop recorder."

A few years ago, I had the loop recorder removed.
The battery had died, and my cardiologist believed
we'd solved the mystery of my wackadoodle heart.
That left a scar— an "equals" sign above my heart.

If I wear a deep v-neck or strapless shirt, it's noticeable,
but I don't mind. I like the way scars look—they tell a story.
What I do mind is the seatbelt: how the strap rubs that spot,
irritating the scar tissue, driving me batty.

Most days, I forget the scar exists. But when conditions are
just so, I'm reminded—a small ache, a sudden flood of memories:
ER visits, ambulance rides, my son's terrified face as he watched
me fall in and out of sudden, violent seizures that one night.

My mom once told me grief is like a ball in your mind:
huge at first, constantly banging against the walls of your thoughts.
Over time, it shrinks, but never disappears. A stray scent,

a familiar song—and BAM! The ball rolls, bumping the walls,

sending a bolt of pain through you...much like my scar, unnoticed
until something rubs against it the wrong way.

We're all wandering this world with scars and grief,
stumbling through our daily routines. That's why I wrote this book—
to remind you you're not alone. Your grief, your scars, your fears—
they all matter. You matter.

I'm afraid to release this book. The world feels so cruel lately.
I fear judgment, mean words, irrelevance. But more than that,
I fear losing myself. I fear being swept away by propaganda,
war, or the slow erosion of our liberties.

I just want this world to be lovely. I want neighbors to
share sugar and strangers to feed pigeons in the park.
Every night, I pray (to someone—I'm never quite sure who)
that the world will heal. That we will heal. The good and the bad alike.

I know it's a pipe dream, but I believe in it anyway.
I believe in happy places and big hugs and fairness for all.
I believe hate and injustice could become just another ball of grief—
shrinking, shrinking, until one day it's just a lesson in a history book.

And then, finally, we could comfort each other.
I know this sounds naive. I know my softness makes me vulnerable.
But I don't want to harden. I want to hold tight to my
high expectations, because we—humans—are capable of greatness.

75

Strong Heart

Being soft isn't weakness; it's courage.
In a world that rewards cruelty,
softness is bold, brave, and daring.

Yes, you're vulnerable to being hurt—
but when someone screams in terror,
falling to what they think is their end,

your softness can catch them, hold them,
care for them, love them, and guide them
until they find their strength again.

Place your hand over your chest.
Feel your heart beating, strong and steady.
It's been with you from the beginning
and will carry you to the end.

It is a lovely, strong heart.

Strong Heart
A Story of Coming Home

* * *

All These Photos

Hi reader. I thought you might want to know, seeing as I've talked quite a lot about my gardening in this book, that every picture of a flower in here, I took from my garden, with my cell phone. Aren't they lovely? I am no expert in photo editing, so please forgive my rough background removals.

Here's one more picture for you: this little baby personally sampled some of these flowers. I wish I knew their honest reviews.

Thank you for reading my book.
I am honored, humbled, and grateful.

And a special thank you to:

- Mom and Dad, for putting up with me, loving me, and never giving up on me.
- Joey, for every single honest talk; especially the ones about how I have all those tools in my toolbox.
- Lynne Dozier, who I still feel walking beside me and who (for me) normalized and celebrated the soft heart.
- Greg Oaks, for helping me finally find my voice.
- Krista, for every last meatball that fueled this project.

- To the boys of my dedication page for which there is no amount of space in the world to adequately express my gratitude for the love, support, and excitement you've shared with me every single day. Heaven exists and it's sitting on the couch in-between you two, listening to records, playing dunge.

- And finally, to everyone who's read my blog, sent notes, bought my books, made me laugh, made me cry, picked up when I called, and believed in me.

I am so, so grateful.

About the Author

Jess is a writer and storyteller with a gift for capturing the raw, unfiltered emotions of life. Through poetry and prose, she explores themes of **resilience, motherhood, anxiety, and the human experience** with honesty and depth.

In addition to *Strong Heart*, Jess is the author of two beloved children's books, *Tink the Bravest Donkey* and *Will You Be My Val-Equine?*, stories that celebrate **courage, friendship, and kindness.**

When she's not writing, Jess can often be found with her hands in the dirt, nurturing her garden and finding joy in the natural world. A devoted lover of all creatures, great and small, she believes fiercely in **standing up for the little guy**—whether human or animal—and strives to bring compassion and empathy to everything she creates.

Her writing is a testament to the power of words—to heal, to empower, and to remind us that even in our most vulnerable moments, **we are never truly alone.**

www.ingramcontent.com/pod-product-compliance
Lightning Source LLC
LaVergne TN
LVHW021952060526
838201LV00049B/1679